£1.99

e Corgi Series

SHEENAGH PUGH
What if this road

The Corgi Series   *Writing from Wales*

The Corgi Series   *Writing from Wales*

SHEENAGH PUGH

What if this road and other poems

Series editor
Meic Stephens
Emeritus Professor of Welsh Writing in English
University of Glamorgan

Carreg Gwalch Cyf.

ISBN: 0-86381-711-4

Cover design: Sian Parri
Carreg Gwalch Cyf. wishes to acknowledge the help of
Martin Tinney Gallery, Cardiff (www.artwales.com)
in supplying a slide of the artwork for the cover.

Logo design: Dylan Williams

First published in 2003 by
Carreg Gwalch Cyf., 12 Iard yr Orsaf, Llanrwst,
Wales LL26 0EH
✆ 01492 642031   🖷 01492 641502
✆ books@carreg-gwalch.co.uk
website: www.carreg-gwalch.co.uk

Supported by an 'Arts for All' Lottery grant
from the Arts Council of Wales

We wish to thank Seren for their co-operation
in producing this volume and for their kind
permission to include material published by them.

Contents

Contents

Introduction

One of the most distinguished and prolific poets of her generation, Sheenagh Pugh has an ironic wit and a commanbd of imagery that are both entertaining and factually precise. Her poems give delight on a first reading and repay close scrutiny when they are read again and again for their craftmanship and compassionate view of the world.

Much of her subject-matter is taken from history, especially that of the Scandinavian lands where she feels most at home, but she also writes about contemporary matters such as graffiti, the game of billiards, intercity trains, cyberspace, polar exploration, the Lockerbie disaster and the beautiful young men who built the Millenium Stadium in Cardiff. In fact, there is very little in everyday life which escapes her notice and she is able to make poems out of the quiddities as well as out of the major themes of life and death.

Sheenagh Pugh teaches Creative Writing at the University of Glamorgan. She was born in Birmingham in 1950, of Welsh-Irish parentage, and has lived in Wales for many years. At the University of Bristol she read Russian and German and then took up a post as a civil servant in the Welsh Office. A selection of her translations from the work of German and French poets appeared in her book, *Prisoners of Transience* (1985), with which she won the Babel Prize for Translation. She has also published two novels, *Kirstie's Witnesses* (1998), which is set in her beloved Shetland, and *Folk Music* (1999), a tender but powerful story about the fate of women in a strictly regulated community which bears some resemblance to 19th-century Christian Armenia.

Her poetry is various and multi-layered from the simplicity of folk-verse to longer sequences with a philosophical underpinning that give them a substance seldom found in contemporary writing. At the heart of her poetry is a concern for language, its subtle nuances and capacity for expressing the pathos of the human predicament in an understated but highly effective way. It does not try to put the world to rights, nor is it used for a display of private emotion; rather, it seeks to explore the individuality, sometimes the eccentricity, of other people, in ways which reminded one critic, D.M. Thomas, of the Russian poets Akhamatova and Pasternak. That is high praise when one considers Thomas was commenting on her first book, *Crowded by Shadows* (1977).

Since then Sheenagh Pugh has gone on to write nine collections of verse, including *Selected Poems*, published in 1990, which also includes about two dozen new poems which are among her finest work. Her first major book, *What a Place to Grow Flowers* (1979), was followed by *Earth Studies and Other Voyages* (1983) and *Beware Falling Tortoises* (1987), of which the very titles suggest the range and originality of her poetry. There is a serious tone to many of these poems: one examines the nature of dictatorship, another the obscenities of torture, another the Dieppe raid and several the effects of pollution on the world's ecology. But always there is a playful, wry awareness of the incongruous and the astonishing: in one poem Mozart plays billiards, in another Guy Fawkes has a girlfriend, in another Buffalo Bill makes a triumphant return to Pontcanna and in another the last wolf in Scotland addresses the reader from the depths of his loneliness.

Among the important prizes Sheenagh Pugh has won are the Forward Prize and, on two occasions, the Arts Council's Book of the Year award. Her most mature work is to be found in four collections published since the early 1990s: *Sing for the Taxman* (1993), *Id's Hospit* (1997), *Stonelight* (1999) and *The Beautiful Lie* (2002), from which many of the poems in the present book are taken. One of the themes which have caught her imagination in recent years is 'Fanfic', the interface between fiction and reality, on which she is currently writing a book. There is a keen edge and hard light to many of these poems, as if she has absorbed something of the Viking past and the harsh way of life which she admires so much as a regular visitor to Shetland.

One of my favourites in the present collection is the title-poem, 'What if this Road', which seems to be a good way of entering the marvellous but perfectly accessible world revealed in Sheenagh Pugh's work: 'Who wants to know a story's end, or where a road will go?'

A Matter of Scale

He left no grief on Aldebaran;
Cygnus Alpha didn't know the difference
and the long lights of the Milky Way
never paled an instant for him.

Even on his own planet
the most people did not know him;
in his own country, his own town,
his loss was a small matter.

Only in a few lives
is a void left, wider
than a town could fill, or a planet,
or the great sun Aldebaran.

Torturers

So the grandmothers walk, softly, but their black
outlines are hard in the sun, to the big house
of the president, and they demand the children
of their dead children. In voices like ash,
white and brittle, they explain that the torturers
from the last regime, when they had quite finished
playing with someone, and put them away
for good, would not infrequently find
infants left over, and would take them
home to their wives: loot.

The president is a humane man,
and not a little intimidated, besides,
by the vast loss frozen in their faces,
and he says, certainly he will try to find
what's theirs. (To bring the torturers to account
is proving beyond him; where's the evidence,
the witnesses are dead, and anyway
he'd lose half the army . . . But to give back
the old women's grandchildren is justice,
for once, at a bargain price.)

So here and there, in a comfortable house
in the suburbs, some boy tries out
a new name on his tongue. The man
he has been calling father forced the screams
from his father; planted the electrodes

in his mother . . . And carried him home
to feed; play with. He tries saying: torturer,
but fails, because, when you come down to it,
torturers are human like any other men,
and this man loved him.

Filing the Queen of Scots

The Queen of Scots
lamented much, in her captivity,
her billiard table, impounded
during her travels.

Her impassioned request
through official channels
about the *table de billard*
must have paid off, at last,

because her dead body
was wrapped for burial
in the green cloth.

The Queen of Scots
was unusually tall
and slender: she must have had
a good reach.

The historian notes her taste
for risk, her misspent youth,
tut-tuts: files her tidily
under 'queens: bad'.

But every act of filing
is a choice, and sometimes, in truth,
a cock-up: she just belongs
under 'billiards players: early'.

The Haggard and the Falconer

To make a hawk, he sits up and starves
with her; stays with her through the pangs,
the hooded blindness, the sleeplessness aching
in the bones: three days and nights. The effect,
oddly, is to bond them, as torturers
the world over could tell you. Afterwards
they're a team: she'll fly for him
and her own pleasure, wear his colours,
take food from his hand, save
her meat for him.

       There are some, though,
that will not, and until she flies,
he has no way of knowing. A haggard
is a hawk that takes no partner
and shares nothing. Her keen eyes watch
her own chance, the dizzy vertical stoop
from the air, that catches the throat,
is for her; the kill her profit
and her delight.

       So he sits,
light-headed, chilled with hunger,
watching her; awake wondering
what she is, whether he has her.
Some say a haggard is the fault
of the falconer, a want

of devotion; he mustn't fail her.
While she is making, he'll scarcely see
his wife: he went in briefly
two nights ago, before he started
the hawk. His wife, as usual,
lay unmoved, watching him
under her eyelids.

When he has gone, she gives
herself ecstasies, fetching, in the dark,
great raucous breaths, heart hammering,
bright-eyed, exhausted. She could show
him how, but she will not: her love life
needs no helpmate, and if you can fly,
why share it?

The Frozen Field

I saw a flat space
by a river: from the air
a jigsaw-piece. It is green
by times, and brown, and golden,
and white. When green, it gives food
to animals, when golden,
to men. Brown, it is ridged
and patterned, but when white,
a plane of evenness.

When frost touches it by night,
it turns silver: blue shadows
etch the hollows, grassblades glitter
in the grip of silence. It was
in such a place as this,
elsewhere, on the coldest night
of a cold winter, two boys
drove a car, with some difficulty,
over the frozen hummocks, parked
in the breathtaking chill, the stillness
that weighted each leaf down
and shot each other.

It was a place I knew
years ago. I must have seen
the field, in summer maybe,
growing turnips, grazing cattle,

dotted with the white
of sheep, the blue and orange
of tents, and all the while
travelling towards one night
vast with misery, the sharp cracks,
one-two, like branches in frost,
that broke the silence.

Who knows what a field
has seen? Maldon sounds
of marsh birds, boats, the east wind.
The thin wail across the mudflats
is a heron or a gull, not Wulfmaer,
the boy who chose to die
with his king, never having guessed
how long dying could take.

And an oak lives
a long time, but a nail-hole
soon closes. Of all the oaks
at Clontarf, which is the one
where Ulf Hreda nailed one end
of a man's guts, and walked him
round and round the tree, unwinding
at every step?

The night the boys died,
their field was Maldon was Clontarf,
was Arbela, Sedgemoor, Solferino,

was every field where a moon
has risen on grass stiff
with blood, on silvered faces.
. . . Aughrim was so white,
they said, with young bones,
it would never need lime again:
better not to see
in the mind's eye Magenta,
that named a new dye.

It was as if the field
clenched all this in
on itself, hunched over
the pain of all young men
since time began; as if
every crop it ever bore
crowded in on it: barley, blood,
sheep, leisure, suicide,
sorrow, so much, its being
could not stay in bounds
but spilled out over space
and time, unwinding
meanings as it went.

They tangle around
the field's riddle now: *I saw a stage
for pain, a suffering-space.*
The fine mist of aloneness closed it
in the morning: at sunset
it was flooded with blood.

Thinking such things often,
we should see too much. I see
a picnic place, a playground.
My eyes half-open, I lean
against a tree; hear through the ground
children's feet chasing.
The sunlight shivers: *someone
walked over my grave*. I chew
on a stiff grassblade.

Five Voices

Johann Joachim Quantz, flautist

I met the late Lieutenant quite often
in the Prince's rooms. I should explain
that the King's Majesty never approved
of his son learning the flute. Lieutenant Katte
used to keep watch, and give us good warning
of his approach. It didn't always work:
I remember one time, he leaned
round the door: 'The ogre's coming
on the run. I'd lose that fancy gown,
if I were you.' This was an over-robe
the Prince had on; he threw it in a corner,
and we all started stuffing sheet music
down the backs of sofas. The Lieutenant
couldn't stop laughing: I felt sick
with panic. He gestured at my coat:
'You know red puts him in a bad mood?'
We could hear the King's voice now, bellowing
along the corridor, and the Prince
was chalk-white: 'Katte, he'll smash the flutes.'
The Lieutenant clapped him on the shoulder,
(I could never get used to his lack
of formality, his casual manners).
'It's all right, we'll hide'em.' He grinned
at me, and opened the big wood-cupboard
– half-empty, thank God. I huddled with him

in the stuffy, resinous dark, door held shut,
listening to the bedlam. Mostly shouts
or thuds, as the King fetched some book a kick;
once there was a great crackling sound
and an odd smell. The Lieutenant nudged me
and whispered: 'He's pitched the dressing-gown
on the fire.' His eyes gleamed: I swear
he enjoyed the danger. I was rigid,
my palms hurting where the nails dug in,
if only he doesn't look in here.
Catch me in a red coat again,
or passing the time of day with princes
and mad officers who can't stifle
inapt mirth . . . He was still convulsed;
my hand itched to hold his mouth shut
(is that etiquette, in a wood-cupboard?).
It seemed an age before the door slammed
behind the King, and we stumbled out.
I had cramp in both feet: he was still laughing,
until he saw blood on the Prince's mouth.
That sobered him cold enough; his face froze
like a hard winter. Myself, I took my flute
and my departure. I'd had enough
of the quality. If I think of him now,
he's always laughing in the dark.

Peter Keith, ex-Prussian Army officer

Damn beer's flat. A man might as well
be in the army. God, I don't miss that.

I never had any dreams of glory,
but in Prussia, a man had no choice;
the whole bloody country was a barracks.
I was born to it too, but . . . I don't know,
my people weren't native Prussian, you see;
just Scottish adventurers who fetched up
in foreign parts. I've never felt at home
anywhere, so the idea of exile
didn't worry me, not that I ever thought
it would come to that. Well, would *you* credit
a crown prince who planned to skip the country?

Oh, he had good cause, no question.
I was his best friend, bar his sister
and Katte; and not a day went by
that he wasn't shouted at in public,
kicked round the carpet, mocked, whatever
took the old goat's fancy. I'd not have stayed
at home for that, but then my father
wasn't the king. *Nobody* walks out
on a kingdom. When he asked me and Katte
to plan it for him, I really thought
it was just a dream; it'd keep his spirits up
maybe, but come the day, he'd think again.
I didn't do much: arranged a few horses.
It was Katte, with his class, his gift
of the gab, who spoke to the embassies,
squared the French. And I never thought
he meant it, either. I mean to say,

he *was* army, a field-marshal's grandson,
for all his books and music. Besides which,
he never sounded serious about anything
for long. I've heard him spend half an hour
proving God didn't exist; he'd have talked
the Pope round. So I asked: since when
was he an atheist, and he grinned: 'Since
it got fashionable.'

                    It was one day
I went to his rooms: I think, to borrow money,
and I stopped outside because I could hear
a woman: aha, the usual, I thought,
but it wasn't. This was a lady, speaking French,
arguing with him, and I knew the voice.
'It will never work; you must talk Friedrich
out of it' – and it came to me then,
it was the princess. She was very angry;
Katte was trying to laugh it off,
and they say she was sweet on him, you know:
'If you think a prince's friend walks safe,
you're wrong.' And then him, stung for once:
'If I die, it will be in a good cause.'

Die? I damn near did. I sat on the step.
God, he's right, we could; it's desertion,
treason, what have you . . . My mind was
                          whirling;
it was happening, the fools were going through

with it, and I wanted out. *She* knew;
who else? The old bastard had spies
all over the household. Good cause bedamned:
if I die, there'll be nothing good about it.
I'd have run that night, but I was too scared
to make my mind up. I hung around
a few days, biting my nails, till someone
tipped us the wink that it was all up,
and I rode straight for the border.

                    Why Katte didn't,
I can't think; maybe there was some girl
he had to say goodbye to, or maybe
dying in his good cause appealed to him.
He did it well, from what I heard. Here's to him.
This beer isn't as bad as I thought:
I must be getting used to it.

Georg Lisiewsky, *portrait painter*

I know that head. I've had the brow
in my calipers, I know its exact span.
I know how the eyelids half-close
in mockery. I know which colours to mix
for the pale tint of the hair: I know
just how much to darken it for the lashes.
There's a grin that starts at one corner
of the mouth, and when he speaks,
the head tilts slightly back on the neck.

On the neck . . . dear God, how long
are they going to leave it there uncovered?
I have never seen anything so wrong
as that head lying alone, apart
from the slumped body, arms flung out
at odd angles, and nothing as it should be.
I couldn't get the arms right: three times
I painted them over, and the natural line
still wouldn't flow, under that uniform.
It worried me: him too. I recall
our first sitting: 'I want it done soon,
and done right.' He was easy-going
in most ways, but he said that
in dead earnest. I wondered why
so urgent, such a young man as he was,
with all the time in the world.

                    The day I told him
I had the face finished, he came round
and looked a long, long time. He nodded
in the end: 'Yes, it's good, it's like.'
That was praise, from him, though he seemed
quiet rather than pleased. He stood still,
just looking. 'I'll be young a long time,
thanks to you. But the arms are still wrong.'

It was next day, out shopping
in town, I heard he'd been arrested.
Treason, desertion, I don't know. I thought

what'll happen to him, and then
if he dies, who'll buy the picture?
I followed the trial, the sentence, waiting
for a reprieve. One day, I heard
two officers talking: 'He was warned, you know,
the day of the arrest; he should have been
long gone, but the fool hung around.'
'Some girl, was it?'

                    I nearly said: 'no,
he just wanted to see the arms put right.'
But I don't know that. And now they come
with a cloak, a deep splash of blue,
and drop it over the awkward wreck
of limbs, over the fair hair tied back,
and I'm not the man with the skill
to put him right now.

Colonel Reichmann, commanding at Küstrin Gaol

I beg to report that the execution
of Freiherr Hans Hermann von Katte,
formerly lieutenant, was carried out
yesterday, November sixth, according to orders,
at Küstrin. As His Majesty wished,
the Crown Prince witnessed the event
from his cell window. Indeed, as the prisoner
was escorted to the block, His Highness
called out to him: 'Katte, pardonnez-moi.'
The prisoner replied, also in French,

28

that there was no need, and that death
would be no trouble. He then walked on
with the guard, exchanging pleasantries
as if nothing were amiss. All witnesses
were moved by his demeanour. He was quite calm
throughout the execution, which proceeded
without a hitch.

        As had been ordered,
the body was left, uncovered, for some hours
on view, before the family were permitted
to remove it. The prison guards inform me
that the Crown Prince fainted three times
in the course of the afternoon, and remains
in great distress. Everything has been done
exactly according to His Majesty's wishes.

Theodor Fontane, novelist

It was a chill day. We waited, huddled
and stamping, outside the big house,
while the servant hunted up the key.
He took us over the road, around the back
of the church, through long wet grass
to a small, squat, red-brick building.
There was nothing romantic about it,
no following a light down dark steps
into a crypt; he just unlocked the door
and there they were, the carved stone tombs,
cold and ornate. He pointed them out

to us: the general, the field-marshal,
knowing which one we'd come for.

You must look in the corner for the bad boy
in his plain wooden coffin. He has been
on his own ever since he came back,
by night, unannounced, without ceremony,
to be hushed up. Yet, ever since,
visitors have come calling on him
at the back of beyond. They take relics,
if they aren't watched: all the teeth
are gone, and the vertebra from his neck
that bore the sword-cut; some Englishman
made off with that, our guide told us
over his shoulder, keeping a sharp eye
on the white jumble of bones, the bright swathe
of hair still tied in its black ribbon.
I'd not have thought dead hair could gleam gold
like that: burnished armour, celandines
in March? I'll find a likeness later.

He was no great beauty, though. I've seen
his portrait, done the year he died.
A face neither handsome nor ugly;
witty, a little arrogant perhaps,
but very bright.

Lieutenant Hans Hermann von Katte,
born 28 February 1704; executed 6 November 1730.

Sing for the Taxman

If that's a sea of faces,
the wind is your voice,
patterning them with light,
singing up a storm
night after night.

What takes you out there still,
and you an old man? When you wake
on the tour bus, stiff, your back aching,
and home doesn't call, and all you feel
is a longing to draw the tides again
in the next town: what sort of man?

Fifty-eight, looking ten years older,
ten good years, and what's to do
but to get your band together and go

on the road again, while the road's still there,
while there's still somewhere you haven't been?
And they say you're singing for the taxman,

that a decade's dues slipped your mind,
so he's letting you tour to raise the wind.
And it could be; yet who, hearing,

could ever suppose you had a choice;
or could do anything but sing,
as long as the words were there, and your voice?

Iron hair tied back, Indian-fashion
in a headband from the crag face,
black eyes in grey rock, thinking
pain into music.

It was no otherwise
with old Egil, staring out
at his son's killer, the sword
idle at his side: *how can I fight
the sea?*

It moved in him: loss
and sorrow, their tides tugging
his feet, battering away
at the brittle sandstone.
*What am I but rock,
numbed and senseless,
written on by weather,
rain-pocked, salt-eaten . . .*

And the words flashed in the air
like sun off metal, like pure joy
of craft, as they settled
into his pattern.

He was a fighter, a hired sword,
loud drunk and angry silent,
sharp-tongued to kings, dumbstruck
with a woman. You and the boys
would have loved him: he was Pancho,

all the outlaws, the stranger from Blue Rock,
the highwayman come back.

And he could write it: oh yes,
somewhere behind the black brows
it all boiled down
to the bones: the shape of a battle,
a friend set in the wrought silver
of praise, the aching space
where a son was.

Once, too, he sang for the taxman,
ransomed his head from a king
with a cold catalogue
of kennings: *take your pick, Eirik,*
we both know I didn't mean
a single glittering phrase, but Christ,
can't I craft them, just!

Many men on Vin Moor
heard the curious hiss
of arrows, saw blood ribboning
through the river, iron flaming blue
in a man's hand: only one
knew the words for it.

The words for hurting, for missing
a friend, or wanting a woman,
for hating or being happy.

It was a language he spoke;
it came natural, as music
comes to you. I've seen you on stage,
shaping some thought as a guitar chord,
a pause, a slight catch in a word;
translating into the fluent rasp-edge
of your voice.

          This is the language
that few speak, and all recognise:
that happened to me; that's just how it is . . .
that's the way I'd say it, if I could.

Egil rocking his grief
in the dark, taking no food,
being nagged to live: *why,*
with Bodvar drowned?
And his daughter, snapping back:
'my brother needs
a song, and who else
knows the words for it?'

What was I given
that had to be paid
with such a tax?
What but the gift
to grieve aloud, to hold him
in words, to put shape
on my thanks, and my hate?

Sing for the outlaws: sing for the man dead
on Christmas morning, for the kiss of Pride
that killed prejudice, for the Cherokee
in your blood, and the time-stranded cowboy
in your heart. Sing for the whiskey river
and the weed high, for the old Martin guitar
you loved so much and wore a hole in,
and it still played sweet: sing for the long pain
in your back, for whatever makes pain speak,
whatever makes grief delight in music.
Sing because you're the best, because you can,
and sing – why not? – for the taxman.

Climbing Hermaness

Burrafirth

Turn left at the northernmost
village, and just go west
until west runs out. The road
ends with Burrafirth.

At the end of all things
there is a flower meadow,
a great meadow enamelled
with rose-root and red fescue,
a meadow of eyebright,
moonwort and tormentil,
a meadow of black cattle
wading through sunlight
and the scent of thyme, a meadow
with a salt edge, bright colours
blurring into shingle,
a meadow between two shoulders,
huge and green, hunched each side
along the glittering firth:
Saxa Vord and Hermaness,
shrugging at the Atlantic.

There is a great longing
to go no further, to be
beguiled, like the voyagers
of legend. *Why go west,*

the sweet whisper runs, *ahead
are dragons*, and someone leaves
the quest, to wander for ever
in the meadow of heart's ease.

But most go on,
shouldering their gear, looking
back at the jewelled grass,
because beyond the west
there is still a way westward,
because there is Hermaness
to climb: the last cliff
on the last island.

And they start upward, watched
by the incurious cattle
on the beach, munching blue gentians
that taste of salt.

Hermaness
The path is not, at first,
steep, more like a stroll
in the sun. When we look down,
the dust seems to glint: a child,
entranced, squats, pouring it
over his hair in handfuls.
The parents groan, but he rises,
holding both hands up, clean,
and glittering . . . There are gasps,

then explanations: gneiss,
silica, serpentine; guidebook words
put things in their place. Ahead,
the child with the sparkling hair
touches a silvered finger
to his mouth, tasting the wonder.

The mountain sounds
with life: little peat-burns
mutter underfoot, ribboning
the rock; grasshoppers whirr
like power-lines. The path
is mined with rabbit-holes
and black moths that start
out of the heather. Or a patch
of ground opens its eyes, gazes
gravely up, while the mother
circles overhead.

The climb so slow,
it is a small shock
to look down at black dots
browsing in the meadow.
There is mist ahead,
where the mountain curves up
into a steep green wall.
Across the firth, the crest
of Saxa Vord is drowned
in whiteness; now and then,

when it swirls back, great domes
and towers appear briefly
and bright: the caliph's palace
of the air force, listening
from their outpost, scanning
the ocean for enemies.

It is a hut
on the edge of sight
we have to make for,
a smudge on the green slope.
Sometimes the path, or the mist,
dips, and it isn't there:
when it comes back, it never
seems any nearer.

In the dips are patches
of bright treacherous green,
that give underfoot,
sucking. The path stumbles
between heather-clumps; sometimes
an old plank wobbles
across quagmire. Either side
is the pale fluff of bog-cotton;
the sundew, that feeds
on flies; the spotted orchids,
just out of reach. *And do not,*
on your quest, go aside
from the path: all adventurers
get warned about that.

So long looking down,
picking the way: when at last
the ground firms, it is like freedom
to see the firth, the shining
sleeve, pleated with ripples.
Look back: the meadow
is long gone, closed off
behind cliffs, their crevices
lit with sea-pink and the white
of kittiwakes.

The climb to the hut
is steep now, no path trodden,
too few come so far. The safe way
is marked with posts; you fix
the next in your eye: *I'll make it
that far*. The pure air rasps
in the throat; all adventurers
lean on that wall, as if
there were nothing left
to take them on,
till someone says: *right,
that's the climb done,
just a bit further north
and we'll be there.*

Muckle Flugga
The marshland is left
behind, and the brown peat-burns.

We are higher here than snipe
or pipit, higher than butterwort
and yellow asphodel, higher than water,
except the fine salt spray
that hangs in the air.
Colours are colder: squill,
small and blue, like a haze
above the grass. Up here,
the fiddle-scrape of crickets
dies in the level note
of the wind. Even the clamour
from the raucous gannet ledges
drifts up muted.

There is a coldness
of mist, sun-pierced; it swirls
below us, blanking out
the world. Somewhere down there
is the great sheet of brilliance,
the northern ocean, and the rock
of the last lighthouse.
It is not in the tale
that the adventurers come
so far, and cannot see it;
yet it could be. The chill
settles about: there is no reward
for climbing; mountains owe nothing.

But it does clear,
briefly; in a swift moment
it scrolls back, and our eyes search
the blinding brightness for the black
of Muckle Flugga. And we see,
just for an instant, the tower
gleaming through rags of mist.
And beyond the last lighthouse
is the last rock,
the Out Stack, and beyond that
the resplendent sea. And when
the mist pours back, it is almost
welcome, in that place
of ultimates with no end
but light itself.

The old voyagers
would have set sail, hearts thudding,
for the edge, but we know
there are no edges.
We have outclimbed water and land;
we have come to this place
which is sky-coloured flowers
and salty grass, which is wind
aching in the ears, which is light
locked above whiteness,
and there is no insight, no knowledge
to take back; not the flowers,
nor the rare minerals, nor the black moths.

What lives here is for itself:
it must stay, when we go down
the only way we can.

The Last Wolf in Scotland

I am a wolf. I know this
from way back, when my mother's
hot tongue prickled over the heap
that was me and the others,
as she whispered *wolf wolf wolf wolf*.

There are four kinds: wolf,
not-wolf, wolf-food and hurt-wolf.
Not-wolf does nothing to the world,
wolf-food is warm, floods your throat,
fills your guts with sleep. Hurt-wolf
stiffens hairs, sharpens ears and eyes,
thumps inside you.

Wolf smelled different
from the world. When I was blind,
we blinked our way into a dazzle
of smells: a music, note overlaying
note, but always the deep one
under all.

The other day
I went to drink, and wolf
looked up at me. I'd forgotten
the face. So long, since I touched
wolf. I used to find

tracks sometimes, or fancy I heard
a call at full moon. Never near.

I miss that smell, the gap
in the pattern, the note I can't hear
in the music. I miss fur and tongues
and singing voices. I miss the piece
that fell out of the world.

Book

I am the thought that flies in seconds
through a man's head, and lives for ever.

I am all he knew: I am his words
on the other side of the world,
sounding long after he dies.

I can cure the sick, build bridges,
change your mind, choke you with tears.
I can make a world, and man it.

Give me to a child, I am the ocean
cupped in his hands: I am all the sand
of the beach in his toy bucket.
I am the key to the walled garden,
the magic lamp, the island
where the treasure is.

I am could-be and might-have-been,
the story of the people, the store
of seed-corn. I feed the hunger
that grain leaves keen.

Voices in Mousa Broch

Part I

1994

No-one lives on this island any more,
but all summer, all day when the ferry runs,
the tower is filled with languages: sibilant
Japanese whispers in the double walls;
Dutch gutturals echoing on the stone steps,
French, Danish, nasal New York; they come to
                                exclaim
into the steep height; admire its craftsmanship.

By nightfall they are scattered abroad again,
and the wall, that shammed so dumb all day,
comes alive, chattering, purring, hiccupping,
in a reeking patter of storm petrels;
its night-speech, its true summer language,
whose memory lasts it through the censorship
of snow, and the long monologue of wind.

Part II

circa 1153

To Earl Harald in Orkney, greeting.
There has been no change. We are still outside

Mousa Broch, where we have been sitting
some weeks. In your last message, you suggested

we take it by storm. Have you ever seen
the place? It is a stone tower, quite round,
with walls a yard thick, and one way in.
From its top, look-outs scan the whole island,

which boasts not a bush nor a tree for cover,
and God knows we could do with some, to dodge
the constant showers of arrows coming over.
They are well equipped, if I am any judge,

and well manned. The siege goes on, hampered
by the fact that we can find little to eat
in this bare place. The broch is stuffed with food;
he had it all planned out, I must admit.

We hear your mother singing, quite often:
she once climbed to the rampart, which we
                                    thought
remarkable at her age. The young man,
her lover, was there too, and in shot,

but they held hands, and we dared not chance
hitting her. She laughs a lot, these days,
and looks better. She shouted to me once
from the wall: 'Tell my son I love this place'.

It you were to ask me, I should say
that she was old enough to know her mind;
that I miss my bed; that my farm in Orkney
must be going to the dogs, and that this Erlend

of hers is one damn clever soldier
who would make a useful ally. The chill rain
has soaked into my bones, I shouldn't wonder:
I never want to see this place again.

Part III

circa 909

I can't take my eyes off the fire:
I'm fixed here, staring into the flames,
listening for their soft flap, and the sputter
when someone feeds them. They wrap themselves
round the dark. Eyes scorching, I can forget
Thorir Hroaldsson on the high seas
seeking my life.

Arnor is checking what stores were saved
from the wreck; seeing them stacked
in the rooms – rooms! Scrapes in the wall,
shadows seeping from the thick stone.
The girl in my arm shivers against me:
'They look like troll-holes'.

Her mouth tastes cold and sweet.
Because of her, I am hunted.
I stroke her hair, thinking: *I could die
for this*, and the blonde strands crackle
and burn my hand.

Arnor has posted sentries
on the wall's top, distant as stars.
He grins at me: 'The little folk built
to keep out raiders. Odd, really:
would you think the poor bloody goblins
had anything worth taking?'

She burrows under my cloak,
her numbed fingers nuzzling
inside my shirt; my skin jumps.
Staring beyond the flames,
I see our shadows shift
on the wall: two dark folk
seeking shelter, like us and not like.

Part IV

?

When you stoop in our doorways
you will feel we were small.
Measure our fear

by the wall's thickness.

The gulls that nest
each year where we lived
leave no less behind.
Our stone benches
took no impress.

In the shadows
of low-roofed cells
you guess at us;
around the bends
of narrow stairways.

But all you know
is the hollow in the millstone,
and a white midden
of empty sea-shells.

The Woodcarver of Stendal

'Judas? You want *Judas*? Look,
nobody wants Judas.' But the bishop's clerk
was businesslike, unbudging: 'We've paid
for a full set of apostles, lad,
and we're 'avin' twelve.'

Oh right, no trouble . . . The worst man of all time.
I stare at the harmless wood, trying to see him,
the abhorred face. Ho do you carve evil?
I knew I'd need more than one model
to do him from life.

Anger: veins throbbing on the thick neck
of Master Klaus, who didn't like my work.
The glint of coin in miller Martin's face
as he gives wrong weight: old Liesl, drunk and
                                    shameless,
tugging your sleeve,

offering her blotched body . . . Oh, my neighbours
were a great help, donating their coarse features
to my patchwork. I took the blemishes
of my kind, the worst in all of us,
to bring him alive.

But what happened then? He lloks no sourer
than laughing Liesl; as honest as my old master,

who never paid me short; as sober a man
as Martin, who has eyes for no woman
but his plain wife.

Only a great sadness marks him out,
and that was mine. I scraped my heart
when I planed him. John, James, even Thomas,
they were names, nothing beside this Judas
noosed in my grief.

Jeopardy

FOUR HUNDRED JOBS IN JEOPARDY –
it had to be worth
taking a look. But often,
along the road, he was tempted to stop.

Across Cloudcuckooland, it was free sex
all the way; in Cockaigne
roast pigeons flew obligingly
into his mouth. He could have lain
all day by the lemonade springs
of the Rock Candy Mountain.

But he knew where he had to go.
Oh, the gingerbread houses
were fun, and earning a wage
for sleeping late, and winning
races by coming last. But he knew
Jeopardy was still the place.

And it was; it was better
than all of them. At the border,
gates stood open; guards in deckchairs
glanced up to wave the refugees through.
A gleaming bus whizzed them
into the city, along wide avenues
shaded with plane trees, past parks
and playgrounds. He wandered clean streets,

shaking his head, gazing up
in awe at the crystal windows
of the great libraries. He breathed air
with no aftertaste, enrolled
in an evening class, found himself
a National Health dentist.

All night he lay awake,
wide-eyed, knowing he'd travelled,
at last, out of the world.

Captain Roberts Goes Looting

It's best when they surrender. No time wasted
on violence: just a few swift kicks
to the officers' groins, for luck, and straight on
to serious matters.

An ox-roar: Valentine Ashplant's voice;
he's found the rum. Young Bunce is slashing bales
of silk to bright shreds. And the captain strolls
to the great cabin,

pauses at the door; breathes in the musk
and sandalwood: these hidalgos do themselves
                                   well,
and there's the china. White, fluted eggshell
you can see through;

he strokes it gently. *We had some of this*
at Deseada: Val Ashplant smashed the last.
(He's bellowing again: found the sugar
to make rum-punch.)

Will Symson eyes a woman passenger
and meditates rape. But the captain has found
the tea, twisted up in papers. He crushes
a leaf; sniffs. Lapsang,

smoky-scented, and the next is Oolong,
with its hint of peaches. Ashplant's delirious;
found the moidores that'll buy more sugar
and rum. Later,

back on their own sloop, the men cheer
the fire: they love watching a ship burn.
They've hauled over a hogshead of fine claret
to wash the deck;

it's like spilled blood, catching the fire's glint.
Captain Roberts sips peachy gold
from a translucent cup, wondering how long
it'll stay whole.

Two Retired Spymasters

They settled down beside the Suffolk coast,
in the flat lands where men can see for miles
– no hills to hide behind, no tricky forest –
They liked the villagers' polite, closed smiles,

the way a stranger always stayed a stranger.
They used to practise merging with the crowd
of tourists at the festival each summer,
just out of habit; just to show they could.

In the Cross Keys, trying to reminisce
without infringing Acts of Parliament,
they'd talk in hints, pauses, half-sentences.
And sometimes, by the window, they fell silent,

gazing out at the dark, the sundown sea,
and the tired, sunken faces in the glass,
thinking how surely the last enemy
was edging up, for all their watchfulness.

The Fiddler Willie Hunter

1933-1994

An old man is playing the fiddle, perfectly,
slow as pouring honey, all his days
distilled into the notes. This is his tune,
a glass filling with light and white water,
and sons a world away, and ships sailing,
and every fiddler on this windy island,
alive or long dead, who ever made
a lament, and named it for a friend.

He has been dead a month, this old man
who lives in the VCR, whose great gift
can be turned on when I choose to hear
his music. All that learning: all that grief
and joy turned off, as if the perfection
of a life's art were such a little thing
to the indifferent finger on the switch
that flicked him into darkness without thinking.

In his last weeks, racked with the sureness
of death coming, he spent day after day
in a basement room, laying down his music
on tape. He played without food, without rest,
till pain exhausted him; he would sit a moment,
then play again. They say he was never
so fired up, never put such loss
and passion into 'Leaving Lerwick Harbour'.

Last week a boy of fourteen, his pupil,
took first prize, playing the old man's air
to the best judges, but behind his eyes
he was playing to his master . . . And there will
                                        always
be such another, and the strings will always ring,
and a man be remembered in love
who has left a tune, or bent a boy's fingers
to the bow, though it is not enough,

nor the face on the screen that cannot be moved
any more by love; nor the twenty tunes he left,
nor the young pupils. There are still the other tunes
his mind never shaped, and all the pupils
who never knew him. Those he lived among
will keep him, because they were not done with
                                        him,
and would never have flicked the black switch,
being more generous than gods, or death, or time.

This Basement Room

This basement room. No sun gets in.
Its walls are soundproof. Outside,
the air reeks of fish, a raucous scrum
of gulls goes down on the harbour scraps,
and your wife's shoes clatter on the flags
as she hums your tunes. You wouldn't know.

The light slips by: six hours a day
in the northern winter. July nights
will be blue, uncertain, sun dawdling
on the sea's rim, no-one going to bed,
but you know you'll be dead by summer.
This basement room: hour after hour

you make music. The blank tapes fill with tunes,
tunes that waited, these many years,
while you ran the laundry, drove taxis,
fed your family. You're no Gauguin;
you were too good a man to be free.
The light slips by, but what is left,

all your life, now, belongs to you
and your fiddle, and its loosed voice.
One bright morning, you felt guilty:
asked your wife if she'd like to go out,
spend time with you, and she answered:
'You make music: I'll bring food.'

Your death coming set you free.
For all the pain, your bow-arm
flexes easy as ebb-tide
over the notes, easy as a man
coming home after years away.
All your life you wanted this:

this basement room. The waiting tunes
belong to you, and all your life
fills the blank tapes. She brings you food
and sets you free. For all the pain,
she hums your tunes. The light slips by.
Your death coming, you make music.

Fellow-Feeling

He was South Efrican, with that eccent
you can't mistake:
he sold cigarettes to the Third World,
and his talk

was all markets, profits, gross.
He had no problem
with lung cancer; he said politics
wasn't for him,

though he did think of emigrating
'if power were to get
into the wrong hends'. I couldn't take to
a man like that;

we'd nothing in common, except happening
to sit so close
at the snooker. Until the young player
passed next to us,

and my guts twisted with wanting
to stroke his hair,
and run my fingers along his spine's curve,
and I saw my neighbour,

white-knuckled, hungry eyes aching,
fixed on the remote
beautiful face, and I nearly said:
'hey, you too, mate?'

Brief Lives

Papa Stour

An island huddles against the gale
like a hunched shoulder. Fleece, manes, hair,
grass, tears: all streaming.

Trudging against it, eyes down,
fixed on the ground. It's moving;
flakes of ash scudding seawards

then, suddenly, lifted
on a gust, tossed high. They're moths,
hundreds, pale see-through scraps

of airmail. They can't cling
to grass or stone; everything loose is leaving.
They can't steer,

can't assert themselves on a sky
that's pure movement. The wind is full
of waste paper,

brief wordless messages
fluttering out unread
over the Atlantic.

What If This Road

What if this road, that has held no surprises
these many years, decided not to go
home after all; what if it could turn
left or right with no more ado
than a kite-tail? What if its tarry skin
were like a long, supple bolt of cloth,
that is shaken and rolled out, and takes
a new shape from the contours beneath?
And if it chose to lay itself down
in a new way, around a blind corner,
across hills you must climb without knowing
what's on the other side, who would not hanker
to be going, at all risks? Who wants to know
a story's end, or where a road will go?

Stonelight

'Not the frailest thing in creation can ever be lost'
– George Mackay Brown

Each stone happens
in its own way. One stands
true in a house-wall.

Anger quickens another: it flies,
fills a mouth with blood.

Shaped and polished, one shines
in the eyes of many.

One seems inert, earth-embedded:
underneath, colonies are teeming.

But the best are seal-smooth,
and the hand that chose them

sends them skimming, once, twice,
ten times over the ocean, to the edge

of sight, and whenever they brush the water's
                                                    skin,
an instant is bruised

into brightness. The eye flinches. When they sink,
if they sink, the light they left

wells out, spills, seeds itself, prickling
like stars, on a field that never takes
the same shape twice.

Envying Owen Beattie

To have stood on the Arctic island
by the graves where Franklin's men
buried their shipmates: good enough.

To hack through the permafrost
to the coffin, its loving plaque
cut from a tin can: better.

And freeing the lid, seeing
the young sailor cocooned in ice,
asleep in his glass case.

Then melting it so gently, inch
by inch, a hundred years
and more falling away, all the distance

of death a soft hiss of steam
on the air, till at last they cupped
two feet, bare and perfect,

in their hands, and choked up,
because it was any feet
poking out of the bedclothes.

And when the calm, pinched
twenty-year-old face
came free, and he lay there,

five foot four of authentic
Victorian adventurer, tuberculous,
malnourished: John Torrington

the stoker, who came so far
in the cold, and someone whispered:
It's like he's unconscious.

Then Beattie stooped, lifted him
out of bed, the six stone
limp in his arms, and the head lolled

and rested on his shoulder,
and he felt the rush
that reckless trust sends

through parents and lovers. To have him
like that, the frail, diseased
little time-traveller,

to feel the lashes prickle
your cheek, to be that close
to the parted lips:

you would know all the fairy-tales
spoke true: how could you not try
to wake him with a kiss?

The Tormented Censor

He sees what is not given to others,
the foreign magazines before they are made
fit for the faithful. He makes them fit.

All day long, he sifts indecent women.
Runner's World, his glinting scissors meet
and part, amputate bare legs and arms.

All through *Hello!* his soft felt-tip is busy
stroking a chador of thick black ink
over celebrity cleavages.

Even in *Woman's Weekly*, some minx
moistens her lips with the tip of a pink tongue:
he rips it out. The whole page.

They all get shredded, the silky limbs,
the taut breasts, flesh cut to ribbons.
He is devout, and keeps none back,

but after work, walking home, if a woman
should pass, decently veiled, all in black,
his gut clenches; he tries not to look,

as the little devils in his mind whisper
what they know, melt cloth, draw curves
on her dark shapelessness.

Graffiti Man

Flint scratched a stick-man
into stone: *me*. A wavy spear
perched on its hand: *me hunting*.

He torched his way across continents,
Als'kander, Iskandar, Sikandar,
founding Alexandrias.

He wrote his name on diseases,
roses and children, scribbled it in neon
across skyscrapers,

spiked programs with its virus.
He sprayed it on ohms, sandwiches,
wellingtons, dahlias, hoovers.

White columns, grey stones, black walls,
heavy with names beyond number.
Such a one died

in war, of AIDS, from old age.
I, Kallaischros, lie
in the restless sea,

no-one knows where, and this stone
lies too, marking the place
where I am not.

Leningrad's gone, and Rhodesia,
scrubbed off the stone.
Ideas are harder

to clean: names won't come loose
from a phrase of music,
a story, a law, a faith,

but you need a keen edge
to carve them. Most settle
for a can of spray-paint.

On every stretch of sand
stick-swirled patterns,
waiting for the tide;

on every snowfield
the definition of footprints,
crumbling in the sun;

on every window
words, fading on the brief
page of mist.

Segunders are named each day,
and if you breathe on the window,
the words come back.

*Note: Lines 17-21 are a somewhat free adaptation of an epigram by Leonidas of
Tarentum from the Greek Anthology.*

The City of Empty Rooms

There's a city above the city, above street level,
above the blankets wheezing in doorways,
above the window-dressers' tableaux
and the 'sale' signs, above the gold lettering
of the third-floor solicitors, higher yet,

the city of empty rooms. They're carpeted
in deep-pile dust, wall-to-wall silence,
cavity isolation. *Secluded residence
commanding extensive views. No parking.*
Pollsters and canvassers don't climb this far;

no census-takers nor rent collectors.
The city in the air was never surveyed,
the *Rough Guide* missed it out; no-one has studied
its population, its mythology.
Up there, anything might be possible:

maybe the hidden roof-slopes are covered
in gardens, maybe the empty rooms are there
for those who need them, and the gentle murmur
from all the eaves: *loving, loving, loving,*
is the voice not of pigeons but of doves.

Pause: Rewind

Nowadays the dead walk and talk
in the wedding video, the camcorded break,

the fuzzed black-and-white of security cameras.
A policeman watches, as two balaclavas

burst, again and again, through the door
of an off-licence, and the old shopkeeper

panics: blunders into a baseball bat,
slumps in his blood. Before things can get

any worse, the young D.C. presses 'pause',
then 'rewind'. And the dark stream flows

into the head again: the old fellow
gets up: the thieves are backing jerkily through

the door, which closes on them. All right,
all tidy. This could get to be a habit:

so many tapes he could whizz backwards.
That bus and bike, speeding to the crossroads,

will not collide: the drunk at the hotel
will stop short of his car: the young girl

will never disappear down the subway
where her rapist waits so patiently.

Pause: rewind. Freeze-frame where you want
the world to stop. The moment before the moment,

before Challenger leaves the launch pad,
before the boat sails or the letter's posted,

before the singer jumps off the bridge,
before you see the face that ends your marriage,

before the pink suit is dyed red,
before a thought is formed or a word said.

The Faithful Wife

My friend was leaning on the shredder; she looked
                                                sick.
She said: 'I just committed adultery'.
I thought: that's a good trick, in a crowded office.
'No', she said impatiently, 'in my heart.

I'd been telling myself for months it was OK,
that I loved his liveliness, his bright mind;
besides, he was gay. It would never get physical.
I just felt kindly towards him, like a mother.

And the dreams could come, no harm. I'd fantasize
him ill, and visit him, in grief, and make
him smile, dry his eyes. But even in dreams
I was never tempted to take it any further.

And then just now, he wasn't even in my thoughts,
and I heard his voice, I think he was asking the
                                                time,
and it slammed into my guts. My arms ache,
and I can't breathe for him. I can't breathe.'

Catnip

Deep inside, licking the pale-spiked bush,
stroking his tongue along the serrated edges

of minty leaves, setting free the scent
and rolling in it, over and over, breathing it

until his whole world is this piercing note
he can hardly hold, a psychosexual high

that sends him skittering, pawing at air,
glassy-eyed, mewing, breathing hard

and fast, till he falls asleep, complete
and exhausted. Hundreds of years ago,

so they say, hangmen chewed this root
before the job, before the careful positioning

of their man, before the sudden jerk
arched his body, before he collapsed limp.

You, my small mutated tiger, chew leaves
for fun only. When you want to kill,

you do it cold sober; you don't ask
the sparrow's forgiveness, and you don't pray.

The Navigator Loses the Sea

Thirty years ago, he wrote the book
of these seas: two hundred years later,

they'll still be using it. Now he sails
as pilot to Woodes Rogers, back on the roads

and channels he once charted, an old man
looking out from the rail, and nothing he sees

is at all familiar. He can't find
the safe route to Juan Fernandez;

he's misplaced the Galapagos. They ask
about Butung. *No, I was never there.*

Later, below, he finds it in his book;
he spends a lot of time learning the names

and places that have slipped from his mind,
hoping to bluff the captain a bit longer.

A navigator who has lost the sea.
In the Cape Verdes, he reads of salt pans,

vast and silver, and his own excitement
at the great birds, more than he could count,

wherever he looked. *'They were like a wall of new red brick.'* He stares at the word,

its arbitrary, meaningless letters,
wondering what flamingos look like.

For further reading

Poetry
Crowded by Shadows (Christopher Davies, 1977)
What a Place to Grow Flowers (Christopher Davies, 1979)
Earth Studies and Other Voyages (Poetry Wales Press, 1982)
Prisoners of Transience (Poetry Wales Press, 1985)
Beware Falling Tortoises (Poetry Wales Press, 1987)
Selected Poems (Seren, 1990)
Sing for the Taxman (Seren, 1993)
Id's Hospital (Seren, 1997)
Stonelight (Seren, 1999)
The Beautiful Lie (Seren, 2002)

Prose
Kirstie's Witnesses (The Shetland Times, 1998)
Folk Music (Seren, 1999)

Images of Wales

The Corgi Series covers, no.11
'Blue Skies' by Ken Elias

Ken Elias

Ken Elias was born in 1944 in the village of Glynneath, at the head of the Neath Valley in West Glamorgan. After attending evening classes taught by Will Roberts he began his art studies in 1965 at Cardiff College of Art and later at Newport College of Art and Design. He studied painting with John Selway and Ernest Zobole, and gained an Honours Degree in Fine Art in 1969. He joined the first M.A. Workshop at Cardiff College of Art in 1985 and was awarded his Master's Degree in 1987.

Since 1970 Elias has exhibited his work regularly in solo and group exhibitions throughout the U.K. and abroad. Recently his work was shown in group exhibitions held in Mortagne-sur-Gironde, France, Vilnius, Lithuania and Chicago in the U.S.A. He is a member of The Welsh Group and the Royal Cambrian Academy.

In 1978 Elias won a Welsh Arts Council Artist Award, and the Editions Alecto Print Award. He was a prizewinner in The Wales Open Competition of 1989 and the Aspects of Wales Competition of 1987.

In the early 1990s Elias moved from his home on

the edge of Glynneath, to live in the middle of the village, in a house opposite the home where his grandmother and maternal relations had lived during the 1950s. Glynneath Park is nearby, where the Miners' Welfare Hall housed a cinema, and where his aunt worked as an usherette. These are landmarks that Elias revisits in his paintings, a landscape that he is continually reinstating. The artist and art historian Ceri Thomas in his essay 'Et in Arcadia Ego' which accompanied Elias's National Library of Wales exhibition in 2001, wrote 'One of the first key paintings is Blue Skies, 1987/2000' because it presents us with what Elias has described as 'the Arcadia of my 1950s childhood'. Luxuriating in an intense and almost Mediterranean light, the world we behold here and in subsequent pictures is a kind of Welsh equivalent to that evoked in Giuseppe Tornatore's 1988 film *Cinema Paradiso*'.

Elias has described his work as 'reclaiming the landscape of childhood with an adult vision' and 'creating a kind of geometry of my earlier life'. The poet and art writer, Tony Curtis qualifies this comment by saying 'it is really a geometry of the heart'.

However, Elias is not concerned with nostalgia or sentimentality. In his book *Imaging Wales: Contemporary Art in Context*, the art critic Hugh Adams writes, 'Elias' work is not simply nostalgia, it contains a slightly corrosive quality and more than a little chill. There is also the curious electricity of their metaphysical dimension, which conspires to suggest that they are not a depiction of real life at all, but life as it is uneasily dreamed. The works are complex, with deep psychological undertones; they possess a freshness and a directness and simplicity of design which takes great nerve. His sensibility has much in common with the best outsider art.'